HANDSOME VICTORY

HANDSOME VICTORY

by Craig Maki

WAX HOUND PRESS

ALSO BY CRAIG MAKI

"Tomorrow Brings Memories – Detroit's First
Underground Record Company"
Wax Hound Press, 2022

"Detroit Country Music: Mountaineers, Cowboys,
and Rockabillies" with Keith Cady
University of Michigan Press, 2013

Handsome Victory

Published by Wax Hound Press
Beverly Hills, Michigan, U.S.A.
WaxHoundPress@gmail.com

WHP-102

ISBN: 979-8-218-83303-9

CONTENTS

For Dennis Coffey, the "Rock & Roll Kid."

"Today, with less game … it has become necessary for the American hunter to again exercise his skill in the art of luring his elusive prey close enough to justify the use of his gun or camera. In days past, hundreds of duck or geese would pass your blind and you could choose your shot. Nowadays hunters may have the opportunity to fire upon only one flight daily."

Shaffer Productions, narrated by Art Mercier, with Russ Gaede. *Game Calling in Hi-Fi, Vol. 1*. Mercury GC-100, 1960, phonograph album.

Preamble

Seasoned record hunters may nod along with the sentiments of the preceding quote — a call to temper thrills of chase with patience, before pouncing on prey (dusty discs) not easily encountered "in the wild" today. In thirty years of chasing records, I learned to ease my expectations while keeping curiosity close, as I found joy often with old, but new-to-me, rocking platters.

Recently, I trained my scope on an authentically esoteric vinyl pigeon hatched in Detroit, my hometown. Just a handful of lucky collectors around the globe have latched onto copies of this promotional 45 rpm disc from used record dealers and second-hand shops. The only eye-witness stories of its recording, set forth by guitarist Dennis Coffey,[1] a member of the Motown Records "Funk Brothers" studio band, intertwined with research Keith Cady and I completed for our book, "Detroit Country Music: Mountaineers, Cowboys, and Rockabillies."[2] A decade after our book's publication, I stumbled upon the lucky breaks I needed to spin the yarn you now hold in your hot little hands — a tale inspired by a record exhalted by music hounds of rock'n'roll, and historical discs made in Detroit, despite its originator, Dexter Shaffer, having little to no name recognition among them.

---

1. Dennis Coffey, *Guitars, Bars, and Motown Superstars* (Ann Arbor: University of Michigan Press, 2004).

2. Craig Maki with Keith Cady, *Detroit Country Music: Mountaineers, Cowboys, and Rockabillies* (Ann Arbor: University of Michigan Press, 2013).

Vic Gallon, Part I

Detroit's concentration of automobile businesses during the early twentieth century drew waves of people from across the world into the region. The variety of new residents' backgrounds ballooned the city's music scene, attracting top-shelf acts of all kinds, from the vaudeville era, and on. Ballroom, night club, radio, and television opportunities made the Motor City an appealing burg where musicians often chose to linger — some for weeks-long bookings, and some for good.

Migrations from the American South inserted a measure of influence into Detroit's music scene, with the blues, and country music contributing to people's acceptance of sounds that developed into rock'n'roll. For example, during the dark days of World War II, the York Brothers, George and Leslie, made records for the small Mellow label in Detroit, with a style mirrored by the first records cut by Johnny Cash, and Elvis Presley for Sun Records, more than a decade later. Originally from Eastern Kentucky, the York Brothers, with a trio featuring acoustic rhythm guitar, electric lead, and a "hot" bass player who often slapped the strings, inspired a local vogue for rocking hillbilly music in Detroit during the 1940s.[3]

In 1954, Kentucky-born Casey Clark, a country musician, bandleader, and disc jockey at 50,000-watt clear channel WJR radio Detroit, spun Elvis Presley's

---

3. Craig Maki, *Tomorrow Brings Memories: Detroit's First Underground Record Company* (Beverly Hills, Michigan: Wax Hound Press, 2022), 77-78.

first Sun records on his weekday programs.[4] The
following year, Clark's friend Jimmy Work, a Detroit
musician (also from Kentucky), got to know Presley's
early manager Bob Neal in Memphis, Tennessee,
while promoting his own country hits on Dot Records, including "Making Believe." Work explained:

*I didn't know too much about [Presley], and Bob Neal
was his booking agent. ... Neal was also a disk jockey, there
in Memphis. So he called me in Detroit, and wanted me to
go on tour — me and Elvis ... We went down to the [Gulf]
Coast and several different places ... But [Elvis] could sell
a song! He made every song sound good. And he had some
records on Sun ... Bob Neal ... he gave me boxes of them
things to carry back to the radio stations [in Detroit], and
the disk jockeys ... I took 'em around to the one-stops (that's
the people that sold 'em to the jukeboxes) ... I went around
and started playing them, and they listened. They'd say,
"What kind of artist is that? Is he country?" I said, "Man, I
don't know. But I tell you what ..." And some of the [radio]
stations, at first, hesitated to play him. 'Cause they'd say he
was rhythm and blues, rock and roll ... So I told some of
'em, I'd been on a tour with the guy ... and his records are
out, down there — But on all the jukeboxes, that's all you
hear, is his records! ... Those jukebox operators, they really
got with it. Then the [radio] stations started playing him ...
So actually, he came in the back door ... Most of the time,
you start from the radio station, down. But ... the jukebox
operators, they really bought his records.[5]*

---

4. Casey Clark, interview by Craig Maki in 1995.
5. Jimmy Work, interview by Keith Cady in 2000.

Young country singers recognized the potential of Presley's approach, and most shelved their cowboy hats, and boots. By 1957, Detroit's rock-crazy kids danced in the aisles at shows featuring local country rockers such as Jack Scott, Johnny Powers, Jimmy Kirkland, and the Detroit west side's "Rock & Roll Kid" Dennis Coffey, who sang and played guitar at David Mackenzie High School sports events.

After a clueless teacher cut short Coffey's first public performance at his school's talent show (he made it partway through Carl Perkins' hit "Blue Suede Shoes" before she shut off his electricity), Coffey organized a small group to play the big beat during halftime shenanigans at basketball games.

Weeks later, Coffey received a phone call at home from a man who introduced himself as Vic Gallon, a local rock'n'roll singer. Unbeknown to Coffey, the 25 year-old Gallon lived at the corner of Linwood and Nebraska, a block away from Northwestern High School, and just a few miles east of McKenzie. "At that point in time, all I was really doing was playing with my band at the basketball games during the breaks," said Coffey. "Other than that, I don't have a clue how he could've seen me."[6] While dishing compliments to Coffey, Gallon asked if he would organize a group of musicians to make a record with him. The teen excitedly agreed, figuring he might learn a thing or two from Gallon's invitation.

---

6. Michael Hurtt, "Gone, Daddy Gone – Detroit Rock'n'Roll Mystery Man," *Metro Times* (Detroit: October 12, 2011). https://www.metro-times.com/music/gone-daddy-gone-2147337 (Accessed 2024)

Julian "Bud" Skinner. *Illustration by Craig Maki*

Bud Skinner, Part I

About six years before Coffey and Gallon met, 20 year-old Julian G. Skinner, called "Bud" by his family,[7] announced to his parents that he wished to pursue a career in audio engineering. Those familiar with the business of recording might have thought it an exciting choice, considering its basis in the field of electronics, and its trajectory for improvements in audio fidelity, tape, and microgroove disc technologies. However, Skinner was born with cerebral palsy, which dampened his eye-hand coordination, and reduced control of his speech, limbs, and hands. With his family's support, Skinner enrolled in classes at Cooley, and Cass Technical high schools to learn the trade. His father, who moved to Detroit from Virginia, worked as an electrical foreman for a railroad company, so he might have contributed his expertise, time, and savings in helping his son build a sound-proofed space, along with a small control room, in the basement of the family's bungalow on quiet Ardmore Street, near Fenkell and Schaefer roads. In 1953, Skinner began promoting his Northwest Sound Company, offering transcription services; and commercial, private, remote, and onsite recordings. His basement studio was reportedly equipped with an array of shiny, new gear worth $4,000 (equal to nearly $50,000 in 2025).[8]

---

7. Obituary notice for Julian "Bud" Skinner, *Detroit Free Press* (Detroit: February 21, 1993. Vol. 162, No. 283), 27.

8. "Triumph Of the Spirit," *Detroit Free Press* (Detroit: January 11, 1953. Vol. 122, No. 251), 16.

An ad in the February 5, 1956, edition of the *Detroit Free Press* printed a photo of Skinner seated at the controls of his disc cutter and tape machine. Its copy began by emphasing Skinner's grit, with a defiant stance regarding his disability:

> *DESPITE CEREBRAL PALSY, Julian Skinner has set up his own sound recording business. The business, called the NORTHWEST SOUND CO., offers complete High Fidelity tape and disc recording service. ... Mr. Skinner wishes contact with non-professional musicians, singers, and song-writers for possible recording and promotion of records.*[9]

Within a few years of starting his business, Skinner built a modest reputation for recording personal messages, events, concerts, church choirs, small groups of musicians — even funerals. He hired a salesman to scare up business, and a telephone answering service. And he began offering packages to tunesmiths that included a recording session, and vinyl records of the results, pressed in small amounts by the RCA-Victor plant in Indianapolis, Indiana (and other factories, later on). By sifting through recent interviews of local musicians, I found Skinner received at least a couple of such orders in 1957. Three particular sessions he conducted that year proved to be not inconsequential to the history of music made in Detroit.

---

9. Advertisement for Northwest Sound Company, *Detroit Free Press* (Detroit: February 5, 1956. Vol. 125, No. 277), 65. Capitalizations presented as originally printed in the ad.

Bud Skinner, Part II

Wade Birchfield, a guitarist who grew up near
Bryson City, North Carolina, on the edge of
the Great Smoky Mountains, moved to Detroit during
the mid-1950s. Birchfield, who often played music
with his twin brother Wiley, wrote "Hit Parade Of
Love," which bluegrass king (also a Detroit resident,
during the mid-1950s) Jimmy Martin cut for Decca
Records in 1956. Encouraged by Martin's recording, Birchfield started his own label from his home
on Detroit's east side, calling it the Wayside Music
Company, presenting bluegrass music on 45 rpm
discs. In May of 1957, a small ad for Wayside appeared in *Billboard* magazine, describing the company's offerings as "Music Blue Grass Style" — the first
time "bluegrass" was referred to as a genre, in print.[10]

The Chain Mountain Boys, a country group
in Detroit led by Marvin Cobb, featuring young
mandolinist Frank Wakefield, cut Birchfield's second
Wayside release,[11] after which the group broke up.
Wakefield joined Jimmy Martin on the road for a
spell, before returning to Michigan, where he be-
friended Buster Turner, and Doyle "Dobbin" Niekirk,

---

10. Advertisement for the Wayside Music Company, *Billboard*
    (New York City: May 20, 1957. Vol. 69, No. 21), 148.
    Neil V. Rosenberg, *Bluegrass: A History*, Rev. pbk. ed. (Urbana:
    University of Illinois Press, 2005), 114, 124.

11. "New Camptown Races" b/w "Tell Me Why My Daddy (Don't
    Come Home)" by Marvin Cobb and Frank Wakefield with the
    Chain Mountain Boys, Wayside W-105, 1957, phonograph record.

[10]

both of whom, like himself, were from East Tennessee.[12] Turner, who also played mandolin, switched to guitar after teaming up with Wakefield, and Niekirk played banjo. Wakefield's imaginitive picking stood out in the trio, and they stirred 'em up with steady gigs at Charlie's Bar in Southwest Detroit, and the You & I, in Monroe, Michigan.

As the summer of 1957 advanced, a third Wayside single appeared: Frank Wakefield and Buster Turner's "Leave Well Enough Alone" backed with "You're The One."[13] Birchfield had recorded the Chain Mountain Boys' disc with his own tape machine, resulting in middling quality. So when he suggested Wakefield cut another record, Birchfield probably directed him to Northwest Sound Company.

Wakefield said he wrote "You're The One," a romantic waltz, and collaborated on the lonesome "Leave Well Enough Alone" with Carace Hutchins, the former banjo player for the Chain Mountain Boys. After learning their parts, Wakefield, Turner, and Niekirk motored from their homes in Monroe to Skinner's lab. "We went up there [Detroit], to somebody's house, in a basement with a recording studio, and made that record," said Turner.[14] "It was just the three of us. And if you'll notice, I played the

---

12. Frank Wakefield, interview by Keith Cady in 2001.

13. "Leave Well Enough Alone" b/w "You're The One" by Frank Wakefield and Buster Turner, Wayside W-150, 1957, phonograph record.

14. Buster Turner, interview by Keith Cady in 2001. Turner's reference to a basement studio in a house points to Skinner's operation, as does the audio quality of the sesssion.

WAYSIDE
RECORDS

Ethelbert Associates
(B.M.I.)
45 R.P.M.

VOCAL TRIO
W-150-A
HO8W-0420
Sterophonic High
Fidelity

LEAVE WELL ENOUGH ALONE
(Wade Birchfield - Frank Wakefield - Carace Hutchins)
FRANK WAKEFIELD & BUSTER TURNER
Instrumental Accom.
Banjo by Doyle Dobbin

bass strings and they put a little more bass on it than ... a regular guitar. So it turned out pretty good!"

Skinner produced a clean, balanced sound, with a tape echo effect for a modern touch. The trio's haunting "Leave Well Enough Alone" included a "heartbeat of Mother Earth" rhythm (think of the beat often attributed to American Indians in old western movies) that Turner beat on the body of his guitar, while Wakefield and Niekirk strummed their instruments in a minor key during the intro, and finale. The trio also sang a refrain of unusual vocal harmony, perhaps inspired by popular music (or jazz). More than a decade later, bluegrass aficionados came to regard the performance as a sign pointing to the progressive future of the music.

Bud Skinner, Part III

In 1957, Jimmy Kirkland, a guitarist and rock'n'roll singer born in the mountains of East Tennessee, and raised in Detroit, shared a recording session at United Sound Systems on Second Avenue with Johnny Powers (born Pavlik, a Michigan native with Polish ancestry) for the local Fox Records label. Kirkland and Powers cut two wild rockabilly discs that, due to Fox's insufficient marketing, failed to catch on.[15] After realizing their Fox 45s were going nowhere, Powers asked Kirkland to help him lay down some new songs at Northwest Sound. Powers planned to use the results as demos for prospective labels, and promoters.

With Powers singing, and playing rhythm guitar, Kirkland on lead guitar, Marvin Maynard slapping an upright bass, and drummer Clark Locker (a.k.a. Johnny Clark), Skinner recorded six rocking tunes in one day: "I'm Walking" (an original; not the hit by Fats Domino, and Ricky Nelson), "Mean Mistreater," "Oh So Far Away," "Someone's Gonna Hurt You," "Treat Me Right" (another original), and a remake of Gene Vincent's "Be-Bop-A-Lula" — which may have been recorded

---

15. "Long Blond Hair, Red Rose Lips" b/w "Rock Rock" by Johnny Powers with the band of Stan Getz & Tom Cats, Fox GB-916/917; and "I Wonder If You Wonder" b/w "Come On Baby" by Jimmy Kirkland with the band of Stan Getz & Tom Cats, Fox GB-918/919 — both issued as 45 rpm phonograph records. Some time after, Kirkland's tracks were reissued on a label associated with *Teen Life* magazine, a monthly tabloid written by and for teen-agers in Detroit that covered popular music, clothes, movies, and teen-friendly events.

as a warmup, as Powers shouted the blues through two verses while strumming his guitar, without the rest of the band. "I recorded those songs in a guy's basement," Powers told me. "He had kind of a crippled hand, and walked crippled. ... I got the old bill of that studio. ... It was twenty ... or ten bucks for that session!"[16]

The tracks caught the attention of Detroit producer Tommy Moers, who offered Powers a management deal. Moers' acumen led to Powers' next commercial recordings, including the savage "Mama Rock," mysteriously released in Australia as by Johnny "Scat" Brown, and "With Your Love, With Your Kiss" for Sun Records in 1959 (issued with his "real alias" on the label). Powers had been desperate to record at Sun since first hearing Elvis Presley's records on a juke box in a Gratiot Avenue drive-in restaurant in 1955.

Kirkland returned to Northwest Sound in 1958 for a session led by a saxophonist. "His name was Tony ... something," he said. "They were done in a basement ... studio that this young boy had. Johnny Powers set that thing up."[17] The group cut several songs with Kirkland singing, and playing lead guitar. The sax player had planned to press a single from the date, but Kirkland never heard about it. "I'm not sure which one on that tape was on the record. I know there was a sax on it," he added dryly. Kirkland took home a tape that day, and after the reel's rediscovery in 2001, the session

---

16. Johnny Powers, interview by Craig Maki, and Keith Cady in 2001. Ten or twenty dollars was affordable for young musicians, compared to maybe twice as much charged by a well-known studio such as United Sound Systems.

17. Jimmy Kirkland, interview by Keith Cady in 2001.

Label of a lacquer-coated disc cut from Johnny Powers' recording session at Northwest Sound Company.

appeared on the compact disc "Cool Daddy," released in 2007 by Rollercoaster Records of England.[18]

Powers canned his Northwest session until the mid-1970s, when fans in Europe helped revive his rock'n'roll career. Some tracks first appeared on Gary Thompson's Olympic Records of Milford, Michigan, then Powers worked with a variety of labels. When heard together in one blast, Powers' echo-drenched tunes emotionalize the eternal book of teen-age passions. Today, one may find titles from the session on fan lists of the best rockabilly from the era — lists that certainly might include: the Vic Gallon session.

18. "Cool Daddy" by Jimmy Kirkland, Rollercoaster Records 3054, 2007, compact disc.

Vic Gallon, Part II

The day Dennis Coffey met Vic Gallon at Northwest Sound, he brought two other musicians for
the recording date. "A friend of mine, Larry Blockno,
who I played with in my high school band, played
drums," said Coffey. "Since neither of us were old
enough to drive, we got a bass player, Lee Stage, who
was about twenty-three. He had a girlfriend who
always carried a .25 automatic pistol in her purse!"[19]
Stage, who played guitar, and bass in country music
bars, was just a couple years younger than Gallon, a
chubby man dressed in dark blue work trousers, match-
ing T-shirt, black shoes, white socks, and dark, combed
back hair. Gallon strummed an acoustic guitar, and
demonstrated two songs, "I'm Gone," and "I Keep
Lovin' You," both of which would achieve a longevity
unimagined by the cool kats gathered around him.

Coffey recalled the scene as a small basement studio with noise-proofing material covering the walls
and windows. Movable panels (known as baffles) were
set up between musicians to isolate the sounds they
made, and a small control booth stood in a corner. "I
can't remember the name of the engineer, but he was
disabled," said Coffey. "Vic just played us the songs,
and we made up parts, and cut the two sides."[20]

Just as Buster Turner's guitar was adjusted to
sound more like a bass at his session with Frank
Wakefield, Coffey revealed, "Lee tuned his guitar

19. Hurtt, op. cit.
20. Hurtt, op. cit.

down to where it sounded like a bass."[21] The similarities didn't end there, as "I'm Gone" began with Block-no thumping away for two meters by himself, much as Wakefield's trio chorded and strummed a "tom-tom" rhythm with their instruments at the start of "Leave Well Enough Alone," before the band jumped into the song. One wonders if someone (Skinner?) contributed this idea at either session, or perhaps both.

Gallon's songs included a rocker, and a slow love song. When Gallon's vocal made room for musical breaks in the uptempo "I'm Gone," the musicians took off like a well-oiled machine, with Coffey busting out licks nicked from Roy Orbison, Carl Perkins, and Chuck Berry records. The band performed "I Keep Lovin' You" with a smoldering tempo, and Coffey's approach admirably imitated guitarist Scotty Moore's bluesy backing on Elvis Presley's records. "I had a doo-wop group first, a Midnighters type thing, with just me playing guitar and four black guys singing," said Coffey. "When I heard [Chuck Berry's] 'Maybellene,' I thought, 'What the hell is THAT?' We had to pay our dues by learning off the records. There was nobody who could teach you this stuff. Roy Orbison, when he was on Sun; [guitarist] James Burton — these guys were inventing it."[22]

Gallon sang "I'm Gone" as if he was Gene Vincent crooning an Eddie Cochran tune, with a clear, nervous voice laying out amusing options for taking a one-way road trip, unless his girlfriend started making with the

21. Hurtt, op. cit.
22. Hurtt, op. cit.

loving. He began half-jokingly, but by the end of the
song, Gallon sounded like he was ready to scram.

> *I got a suit with two pair a trousers, I got a key chain*
> *four foot long*
> *Bought me a brand new back-seat speaker, Radio*
> *settin' on a rock billy song*
> *So you better kiss me mama, You better kiss me sweet*
> *You better kiss me kin'-da strong*
> *Well, you better not let me — Get out of your sight,*
> *or Honey, I'll be gone!* [23]

What to make of a "four foot" key chain? During
the 1940s, a long chain was part of the zoot suit of
nonconformist big city dwellers — long coats with
triple-wide lapels, exaggerated shoulder pads; and
baggy pegged pants gathered with small cuffs at the
ankles, worn with wide brimmed hats. The style first
attracted attention during World War II, when young
American Black, and Latino men wore the oversized
clothing in defiance of government fabric rationing.
In 1957, zoots were considered relics of a bygone
era. Furthermore, in the last verse of the song, a line
describes a buddy's girlfriend as "sharp like a WAC
[pronounced "wack"] on a three day pass," which
refers to the Women's Army Corps, also invented
during World War II. Gallon had lived through the
war years, but as a child. These dated phrases, which

---

23. Dexter Shaffer - Delita Meyers, "I'm Gone" Lyric sheet
(Detroit/Chicago: De-Shaf Music Company, BMI, 1957) The
terms "back-seat speaker" and "radio" refer to an automobile
described earlier in the song.

may have puzzled kids at the time, since rock'n'roll
was all about new music, clothing, dances, and so on,
presented details someone with an older perspective
— perhaps older than Gallon's — might, in an out-
of-touch oversight, have contributed to the song. Still,
because the message of early rock'n'roll was mostly
defined by the rebellious spirit of its performance,
Gallon and the band spread on the attitude as thick
as they could, and "I'm Gone" rocked.

"I Keep Lovin' You" presented a slow-dance
meditation on how the passage of time made no
difference to Gallon's love for his sweetie. Gallon's
warble, seasoned with emotional cracks in his voice,
succeeded in delivering genuine feeling on this number, too. Some folks who've heard both sides of the
record prefer this performance.

> *Well, somebody laughed, Somebody cried*
> *A baby was born, Somebody died*
> *Well, life goes on, I keep love — Lovin' you* [24]

Skinner's use of tape echo effects on the recordings kicked the rhythm up a notch, and the results
sounded clear, and commercial. The band cut several
takes before Gallon found two he dug the most. Coffey had a blast, and said so. Gallon replied he thought
the band sounded great, and hoped they could do
it again, as he handed Coffey his fee. For just a few
hours of picking guitar, Coffey took home thirty bucks,
and the experience set a new course for his life.

---

24. Dexter Shaffer - Delita Meyers, "I Keep Lovin' You" De-Shaf
Music Company, BMI. 1957.

Label of an original Gondola record. Label scheme: light peach/
pink colored paper with black ink.

One of Gallon's records — a custom order of
probably one hundred copies (or fewer) pressed at the
RCA-Victor plant in Indianapolis, Indiana — appeared in Coffey's mail a few weeks later.[25] Above
the label name "Gondola" (meant to be pronounced
gone-dollar?), it read: "Complimentary." And below

---

25. "I'm Gone" b/w "I Keep Lovin' You" by Vic Gallon, Gondola
   G-1414, 1957, phonograph record. These RCA custom matrices
   were stamped in the record's deadwax: H8OW 8799 / H8OW
   8798. The "H" indicates a 1957 pressing.

that: "Dee Jay Special," "Promotion Copy," "Not For Sale," along with, "Vocal By Vic Gallon." Coffey was thrilled to see his name on the label (printed "D. Coffey"), and even more excited to spin the seven-inch disc on his record player.

Gallon phoned Coffey some days after he received his copy of the record, and told him to tune in WEXL radio Royal Oak, that afternoon. Gallon was scheduled to appear as a guest on "Sagebrush Melodies," a popular country music show hosted by disc jockey Uncle Jack Ihrie.[26] When he turned on his radio, Coffey perked up as Gallon announced the names of the musicians who played at the session, and turned up the volume as Uncle Jack gave both sides of the record a spin. "I listened to it, and what a thrill! I'm hearing myself on the radio!" he said.[27] And that was the last he heard from Vic Gallon.

---

26. "Sagebrush Melodies," a daily afternoon show, was popular with country music fans during the 1950s, as it was among only a few in the Detroit area, before radio stations began adopting schedules featuring nothing but country music, as WEXL did in 1962. For more than thirty years before then, the station operated with a common brokered time, or "pay for play," format, with emphasis on religious programming, besides hosting local groups performing folk, old-time, and cowboy music in its studios.

27. Hurtt, op. cit.

Bud Skinner, Part IV

Skinner launched a record label in late 1960 named after his business, Northwest Sound Company, with a pair of 45s featuring Nick Harris and the Soundbarriers, a combo that specialized in rock'n'roll instrumentals. With a style similar to the chart-topping Toledo, Ohio-based Johnny and the Hurricanes, the Soundbarriers included two driving guitarists (one of whom was Harris), a saxophonist, an organist, drummer, and bassist. Vocalist Jimmy Mack "D" sang both sides of Skinner's first outing, a rocking novelty titled, "She's Got It!" (an original; not Little Richard's hit song) backed with the sentimental, "Yes, It's True."[28] As the backing band, the Soundbarriers came across well rehearsed, and again, Skinner achieved magical results at his studio. Shortly after his record's release, Jimmy Mack "D" turned up with a quick review of his disc in, of all places, the small *Enterprise Ledger* newspaper of Southeast Alabama. WIRB radio Enterprise host Chet Smith spoke with the artist in person, and reported, "Jimmy likes the 'She's Got It' side ... we like the other."[29]

---

28. "She's Got It!" b/w "Yes, It's True" by Jimmy Mack "D," Northwest Sound Company NSC-1001/NSC-1002, 1960, phonograph record.

29. Chet Smith, "Music This Week," *Enterprise Ledger* (Enterprise, Alabama: January 26, 1961.), 12. The wife of Johnny Powers' agent Tommy Moers was from Montgomery, Alabama. Moers may have provided an introduction for Jimmy Mack "D" with Smith. Moers, a pianist, appreciated Skinner's skills. In 1961, he and his friend Roy Corwin (née Cohen) made a single with Skinner's Roman label (*see pp. 72-73*). In 2025, Moers' son Ray described Skinner to me as having difficulties conversing, but "a genius in the studio."

The second, and probably best, Northwest
single featured instrumentals "Big Nick" backed
with "Music, Music, Music," a rock'n'roll arrangement of pop singer Theresa Brewer's No. 1 hit of
1950.[30] Prior to this, Harris played with guitarist Al
Allen in the Sounds, another rocking instrumental
group that Allen assembled to promote his 1959
single "Egg Head," which he wrote and recorded for
Carlton Records, while on hiatus from Jack Scott's
band.[31] "Big Nick" borrowed the melody of "Egg
Head" (Harris shared writing credit for "Big Nick"
with Allen, whose surname, Punturi, appeared on the
label), and it opened doors for the Soundbarriers, as
they followed up their Northwest single with more
instrumental rock on the Tee Pee, and Fleetwood
labels of New York City in 1961, and 1963. The band
toured Canada, booking extended engagements in
Ontario and Quebec for a few years, before dissolving
in the wake of the British Invasion. Harris returned
to Detroit, picking guitar, bass, and singing country
music in local bars through the early 2000s.

Skinner also established music publishing companies Skintone Music, and Roman Music (both BMI
affiliates), and pressed a diverse stack of records with
his Northwest Sound, and Roman labels during the

30. "Big Nick" b/w "Music, Music, Music" by Nick Harris and the
    Soundbarriers, Northwest Sound Company NSC-1003/NSC-
    1004, 1960, phonograph record.
31. "Egg Head" b/w "I'm Beat" by Al Allen, Carlton Record
    Corporation 511, 1959, phonograph record. Jack Scott was also
    contracted to Carlton. Nick Harris did not appear on the record
    — Allen said he overdubbed secondary guitar parts himself.

1960s, including local acts performing pop, rock'n'roll, doo wop, instrumentals, and so-called '60s garage rock (*see page 70 for the list*).

No other records or clients achieved success such as the Soundbarriers enjoyed in 1961, although Skinner stayed active through the 1970s. The late Detroit audio mastering technician, Ron Murphy, who worked at United Sound Systems, Motown Records, and other studios, and co-founded National Sound Corporation, and later his own Sound Enterprises, recalled Skinner used an Ampex 351 two-track tape machine. "He also had a little dub cutter [for making reference records], and the studio was just one nine-by-twelve [feet] room, but he did have good ears, and got a pretty good sound for that setup," Murphy said.[32]

By 1980, Skinner's business had run its course. Cassette tapes put personal recording within reach of most people, and compact discs, heralding the new age of digital technology, soon overtook the public's audio media preferences. His father died in 1983, and Skinner left Ardmore Street for a brother's home in Dearborn Heights. He passed away ten years later, at age 62, and, like the 45s he pressed, mostly forgotten. But as revealed by the celebrated Wakefield-Turner, Powers, Kirkland, and Gallon sessions newly linked to this remarkable man, other significant projects may remain unaccounted for, unless former clients speak up, or log books by Skinner himself come to light.

32. Ron Murphy, originally posted on the Soulful Detroit Forum, reposted in 2013 at the That's All Rite, Mama blog, https://thatsallritemama.blogspot.com/2013/02/dean-o-delray-and-his-delrays.html (Accessed 2025)

Dexter Shaffer, Part I

In the middle of May, 1955, Dexter Virgil Shaffer, Jr., and Lillian Delita Myers wed in Angola, Indiana — a small town famous for providing "quickie weddings" that didn't require waiting periods, as states such as Michigan did, at the time.[33] On the marriage certificate, Shaffer's address read Detroit, and Myers' read Charleston, West Virginia — the city where both bride and groom had grown up in, or near. West Virginia's state motto, *Montani Semper Libari* (Mountaineers are always free), seemed to suit these two characters. Myers, fourteen years older than her groom, stood a few inches taller than he. Despite his stature and youth, Shaffer had an outgoing, persuasive demeanor that endeared him to most. He was a salesman with musical ambitions; she a former dancer with years of experience as an entertainer.

Born in 1918, Myers spent her school years performing at community events with literary recitations, singing, and athletics. She probably studied dance as well, because in 1941, she was strutting across stages with her fiancé in a two-person act, "Martez and Delita," performing in auditoriums, vaudeville theaters, and night clubs across America,

---

33. "Indiana Marriages, 1811-2019" *FamilySearch* (https://www.familysearch.org/ark:/61903/1:1:8M3C-7L6Z), Entry for Dexter Shaffer and Eugene Maloy, 14 May 1955 (Accessed 2025). Also in the marriage document: Shaffer's birth date was written 1927, five years before he was born. Myers changed hers to 1920, making her two years younger.

including bills in front of U.S. military personnel, and with stars such as Desi Arnaz and his orchestra, the Mills Brothers, and the DeMarco Sisters. Martez and Delita included synchronized prancing, songs, humor, and — most importantly — outrageous, daredevil acrobatics with Delita balanced in precarious poses atop the hardy cranium of Martez. The pair, described by one admirer as "equilibrists who work to rhumba rhythms,"[34] married the following year, and continued barnstorming the country nonstop.

Born in Mexico City, Mexico, in 1912, Lewis Martinez shortened his family name for the act. Martez and Delita received accolades everywhere they appeared, with frequent nods to Delita's fearlessness, and Martez's abilities to shuffle across a stage while balancing his wife atop his head. In promotional photos printed in newspapers, Martez appeared in a tuxedo, as well as in flashy Latin American shirts, swinging a pair of maracas. Slightly taller than Martez, Myers appeared slim, neat, and glamorous as a movie star. They seemed unstoppable through 1943, when Uncle Sam invited Martez into the U.S. Army. Unable to decline, he left Myers to hoof it in theaters along the East Coast.

When Martez rejoined civilian life in 1946, the pair resumed traveling the theater circuits. In July 1947, they appeared with comedian Jerry Colonna's show at the Circle Theatre in Indianapolis, Indiana,

34. "To Entertain Eustis Men," *Daily Tribune* (Newport News, Virginia: March 17, 1943. Vol. 48, No. 67), 10.

where an enthusiastic reviewer for the *Indianapolis Star* reported, "Martez does a sprightly little dance, with the shapely Delita planted feet first on his head, then does a series of expert maneuvers with Delita doing a head stand on his unyielding dome. The fun-loving Delita can not help tickling his nose."[35] In spite of their success, after the Colonna gig, the duo parted ways — professionally and personally.

Several months later, Martez restarted the routine — professionally and personally — with a dark-haired woman named Lucia. For a few years during the mid-1950s, Martez and Lucia brought a second woman into the act. They kept a "balanced" relationship as professional entertainers well into the 1960s.

By 1950 Myers lived in New York City. A government census noted she dressed hair in a salon, while rumor has it she danced with the Radio City Rockettes. How the talented Lillian D. Myers met Dexter V. Shaffer, Jr. remains a puzzle, but to the story of Vic Gallon, what matters is they got together.

---

35. "Jerry Colonna's Show Is Long On Comedy," *The Indianapolis Star* (Indianapolis: July 25, 1947. Vol. 45, No. 50), 26.

Dexter Shaffer, Part II

A catalog of unpublished music copyrights as-sembled by the United States Library of Con-gress provided a first glimpse of the Shaffer-Myers creative partnership, with a song titled "Fairy Land Of Love,"[36] registered in 1956, and presumably in-spired by their first year of wedded bliss. It's a good bet no one alive today has heard the tune.

The next year, they achieved, in retrospect, lasting glory with "I'm Gone"[37] and "I Keep Lovin' You,"[38] the songs Vic Gallon immortalized at 45 rpm. Ac-cording to a hand-written lyric sheet of "I'm Gone," — probably sent to the record factory with Gallon's order[39] — Shaffer wrote the words, and Myers the music, despite what Dennis Coffey set forth about the band working up the arrangements at Northwest Sound the same day they made Gallon's recordings.[40]

---

36. *Catalog of Copyright Entries, Third Series, January–June 1956* (United States: Library of Congress, Copyright Office, 1957. Vol. 10, Part 5B, No. 1), 53.

37. *Catalog of Copyright Entries, Third Series, July–December 1957* (United States: Library of Congress, Copyright Office, 1958. Vol. 2, Part 5, No. 2), 1239.

38. *Catalog of Copyright Entries, Third Series, July–December 1957* (United States: Library of Congress, Copyright Office, 1958. Vol. 2, Part 5, No. 2), 1217.

39. See note 23. An old wax hound informed me a record collector in Indiana, where the RCA-Victor factory pressed the Gondola discs, found a copy of an original lyric sheet. It included two addresses — one in Detroit, another in Chicago.

40. Coffey, op. cit.

Just after Gallon began promoting his record in Detroit, the guy disappeared. That year, Shaffer and Myers moved from Detroit to Chicago, Illinois, where Shaffer likely used the Gondola 45 to attract the attention of Mercury Records music director Carl Stevens. Mercury was incorporated in Chicago in 1945, and began making popular, jazz, classical, and rhythm and blues discs. The label also promoted country music, and signed rock'n'roll artists after the big beat blew up in 1956. Stevens, born Charles (a.k.a. Chuck) Sagle in 1927, in Aurora, Illinois, studied music at the University of Illinois. He started his own production company in 1958, working with Epic Records artists such as Link Wray, and Ersel Hickey, among others. In 1972 Stevens moved his business to Nashville, Tennessee. By the time he passed away in 2015, Stevens had worked with stars such as the Platters, Bobby Darin, Gene Pitney, Frank Sinatra, the New Christy Minstrels, and Carole King.

As a bandleader and arranger, Stevens backed Mercury artists in the studio. He also orchestrated his own instrumental records, which some classify today "mid-century exotica." His role for Mercury focused on talent based in the Midwest, and it was not uncommon for Michigan entertainers to record in Chicago. For instance, Vada Belle, a country singer from Bay City, Michigan, cut a session at Chicago's Universal Recording Studios in early fall of 1957,[41]

---

41. "Blue Tomorrow" b/w "Gold In My Sunshine" by Vada Belle and the Anita Kerr Singers, Mercury 71210, 1957, phonograph record. Mercury release date on labels reads, "Oct. 2, 1957."

and George Young, a popular Detroit rocker, made
the trip for his only Mercury record, the shaking
shouter "Can't Stop Me,"[42] a few weeks later.

According to Mercury studio logs, Shaffer
himself recorded "I'm Gone," and "I'll Keep Loving You" [sp.] with the Carl Stevens Orchestra on
a day that fell between the Vada Belle, and George
Young sessions.[43] The entry for Shaffer's recordings
declared the tracks "unissued." It appeared right
after a four-song session by Chicago-based pop
singer Nick Noble, who charted hits for Mercury
with "A Fallen Star," and "Moonlight Swim," backed
by Carl Stevens, earlier that year. The Noble session
(also backed by the Carl Stevens Orchestra) that
preceded Shaffer's included "Sweet Treat" and "Halo
Of Love," which Mercury released together on one
disc, October 31, 1957.[44] As for Shaffer's unissued
performances, we now know an audio technician
transferred copies of it to lacquer coated discs.

---

42. "Can't Stop Me" b/w "Come Back To Me" by George Young,
    Mercury 71259, 1958, phonograph record. Mercury release date
    on labels reads, "Rel. Jan. 17, 1958."

43. Ruppli, Michel, and Ed Novitsky, *The Mercury Labels: A Dis-
    cography, Volume II, The 1956-1964 Era* (Germany: Greenwood
    Press, 1993), 114, 115.

44. "Sweet Treat" b/w "Halo Of Love" by Nick Noble with Orches-
    tra and Chorus Conducted by Carl Stevens, Mercury 71233,
    1957, phonograph record. Noble's last successful single of his
    career was the 1978 pop-country "Stay With Me" on Churchill,
    reaching No. 40 in North American country music charts.

Ernie Durham. *Illustration by Craig Maki*

Ernie Durham, Frantic I

In December 1992, rock and soul radio king of platter chatter Ernest Lamar Durham, a.k.a. Frantic Ernie D., passed away at his home in the storied Boston-Edison district of Detroit.[45] His on-air rhyming patter — *"Well howdy doodie, once again, friends! Back on the scene with my rockin' machine! Your ace from inner space! Your host who loves your singing musical entertainment most: Ernie Durham! With nothin' but the best — LATER for the rest!"*[46] — and willingness to spin stacks of rock'n'roll wax made him a duke of the dial in Southeast Michigan, where he hosted radio programs, amateur stage shows, record hops, benefits, and the nation's hottest rock'n'roll acts, beginning in 1949, after his arrival from New York City, via Pittsburgh, Pennsylvania.

Durham climbed to the top of Detroit radio broadcasting during rock'n'roll's breakout years, standing out among the music's early promoters. You could tap any musician or entertainer who participated in Durham's shows, and record hops, or interacted with him on radio, and receive a shower of undiluted praise for the Frantic One. Often referred to as the "nicest man in show business," Ernie D. received multi-page spreads in national music magazines from leading

---

45. Neely Tucker, "Radio legend Ernie Durham dies at 73," *Detroit Free Press* (Detroit: December 4, 1992. Vol. 162, No. 207), 16.

46. Frantic Ernie Durham, *1958 Aircheck*, The Rex Doane Collection, Rock Radio Scrapbook, https://rockradioscrapbook.ca/air1958.html (Accessed 2025)

figures in the record industry.[47] Even Berry Gordy, Jr., the famous leader of Motown Records, cultivated his advice.[48]

When he died, Durham left behind a library of records — most sent to him directly from promoters, and artists — relics from an era when songsters could easily visit with disc jockeys who had freedom to spin whatever grooves electrified their ears, and turned their gears. Before radio stations adopted strict formats, and playlists of musical styles, and titles, dee jays relied on meetings with musicians, record labels (payola? I found no evidence pointing to Ernie D.), distributors, listener feedback, as well as industry magazines such as *Billboard*, and *Cash Box*, to locate the latest popular tunes. Moreover, hosts such as Durham collected records during the 1950s because not all radio stations maintained music libraries.

Many stations required individual producers to sell advertisements to pay for hours on the air, yet Durham's local stardom helped him avoid treading the pavement to sell ads. Smart station managers took care of that for him (in his case, an ad agency served as the middleman), which gave Durham two hands loose to

---

47. "In Small Payment," *Record World* (New York City: Sept. 28, 1968. Vol. 23, No. 1112), 23–29. A seven-page tribute to Ernie Durham, whose portrait graces the cover, describes a special dinner in Southfield, Michigan, set up by music distributors in Durham's honor, and includes best wishes from the likes of Don Robey of Duke/Peacock Records; Stan Lewis of Jewel/ Paula Records; Nat Tarnopol of Brunswick Records; Jerry Wexler of Atlantic Records; Stax/Volt Records, Columbia, and Capitol labels.

48. Tucker, op. cit.

pursue new recruits to his rockin' institute. Durham's early career, from CKLW Windsor, to WBBC Flint, then to WJLB Detroit, functioned within this business model. Even while Durham broadcast through the 1960s at WJLB, the station continued to feature "pay for play" scheduling that included Polish, Italian, and Greek culture shows until 1970, when station owners changed its focus to programming for Black listeners. At that point, Durham had been cruising in the catbird's seat for more than fifteen high-flying years.

After World War II, independent record companies (without ties to the major labels Decca, Columbia, and RCA-Victor) often sent free/promo records to disc jockeys as a way to sponsor special segments. It appears Mercury Records did so in 1950, when Durham and his co-host Tony Vance broadcast the "Mercury House Party" at CKLW radio.[49] Durham likely established a long-term relationship with Mercury representatives, who supplied him the company's latest discs.

Did Vic Gallon give frantic Ernie D. a copy of the Gondola 45? I checked with someone familiar with the sale of Durham's records after his death, but we could not confirm this. However, a twelve-inch lacquer coated disc, most likely cut for review of its contents (in other words, a demo), with no paper labels, and "I'm Gone" scribbled in grease pencil near the spindle hole, was, in recent years, traced back to the Frantic One's trove of tunes.

---

49. Advertisement for the Ernie Durham and Tony Vance radio program on CKLW radio, *Detroit Tribune*, (Detroit: July 29, 1950. Vol. 28, No. 26), 3. The show aired Monday through Saturday, 1 to 2 a.m.

Dexter Shaffer. *Illustration by Craig Maki*

Dexter Shaffer, Part III

Not long ago, Kevin Legg, a nephew of Dexter Shaffer, playfully described him to me as "a charmer and a con, necessary traits for a sales rep. ... Uncle Dexter, or D.V. as he was known, was quite a character, and could hold an entire room captive as he told his stories of the music business, and his youth, growing up in West Virginia."[50]

The son of a salesman who shared his name, D.V. Shaffer, Jr. was born March 29, 1932, in Chesapeake, West Virginia, south of Charleston, along the Kanawha River. His parents brought a daughter into the world two years later, and a 1940 census reported Shaffer Senior operated an insurance office. In 1946, Shaffer's dad died of a brain hemorrhage, and a year later his mother passed away from a severe illness. An older brother, who had grown up and left town, returned to Chesapeake with his wife to look after Shaffer and his sister as they finished school. Or tried to. "D.V. was more than a handful," said Legg. "[He burned] down a house to avoid going to school, one day."

Following his recordings with Carl Stevens, Shaffer hired into the Ram Golf Corporation, a leading supplier of clubs, balls, and accessories. Then he hit a ball no one saw coming: In 1960 Shaffer produced "Game Calling in Hi-Fi, Vol. 1" for Mercury Records.[51] A surprisingly

---

50. Kevin Legg, e-mail message to the author, May 11, 2025.

51. Shaffer Productions, narrated by Art Mercier, with Russ Gaede. "Game Calling in Hi-Fi, Vol. 1" Mercury GC-100, 1960, phonograph album.

entertaining spoken-word album about hunting wild game in America's back country, its stories sparkled with true-to-life tales woven together with instructional lessons. Narrator Art Mercier, a Chicago radio (WBBM) and television (WGN) commentator known for expounding on outdoor sports such as fishing and hunting, delivered a friendly, authoritative performance, with touches of melodrama, illustrated by game calls from Russ Gaede. Tom McNally, a sports columnist at the *Chicago Tribune*, contributed advice to the project, and gave it a plug in the paper that December.[52] In spite of its unique concept and excellence, further volumes never materialized. While at Ram Golf, Shaffer rose to head its national sales, and presumably continued writing songs in his spare time.

In 1968, Shaffer placed a few of his songs with Starday Records in Nashville, Tennessee. Later that year, Starday owner and president Don Pierce (an avid golfer) chose Shaffer to head his song publishing business.[53] Once settled in Nashville, his tasks included hiring songwriters, and persuading artists to record titles Starday had published. Shaffer spent his days running ten miles back and forth between the Starday office on Music Row, the urban heart of Nashville's music industry, and Starday (soon to be known as

---

52. Tom McNally, "Christmas Tips On What To Buy Sportsmen," *Chicago Tribune* (Chicago: December 18, 1960. Vol. 119, No. 51), 77.

53. "Shaffer Heads Starday Publishing Operations," *Record World* (New York City: Sept. 28, 1968. Vol. 23, No. 1112), 58. This is the same edition described in note 40!

Starday-King) Studios and headquarters, north on Dickerson Pike, just outside of the city limits.

Reports on Shaffer's new situation noted he had co-written three recent Starday releases (two with a young writer named William Brown Ellis), including one that sold fairly well: "Frisco Line" by Guy Mitchell,[54] "Country Music Singing Sensation" by Kenny Roberts,[55] and "Wild Wild Thing" by Billy Golden.[56]

Shaffer's biggest song was a folksy ballad that suited the soft sounds of "middle-of-the-road" radio of the time: Guy Mitchell's record of "Frisco Line," which climbed to No. 71 in the *Billboard* Hot 100. Born Albert Cernik in Detroit to Croatian immigrants in 1927, Mitchell left town eleven years later when the family moved to California. After a few years in Los Angeles, the Cerniks settled in San Francisco, where Mitchell sang cowboy songs with Dude Martin and his Round-Up Gang. He served in the U.S. Navy during World War II, and, after the war, worked with big bands. Mitchell's career took off in 1950, when he joined Columbia Records. With guidance from music director Mitch Miller, Mitchell remade country hits

---

54. "Frisco Line" b/w "It's A New World Every Day" by Guy Mitchell, Starday 846, 1968, phonograph record. Also issued on "Singin' Up A Storm," Starday SLP 432 (album), 1968; and "Heartaches By The Number," Starday NLP 2074, 1970 (album).

55. "Country Music Singing Sensation" b/w "Fugitive Of Love" by Kenny Roberts, Starday 851, 1968, phonograph record. Also issued on "Country Music Singing Sensation," Starday SLP 434 (album), 1968.

56. "Wild Wild Thing" b/w "Born Loser" by Billy Golden, Starday 840, 1968, phonograph record. Also issued on "Country Music's Golden Boy," Starday SLP 431 (album), 1968.

Above: Guy Mitchell
Below: Kenny Roberts
Illustrations by Craig Maki

for pop audiences, including Marty Robbins' "Singin' The Blues" in 1956, and Ray Price's "Heartaches By The Number" in 1959, both of which the Miller-Mitchell team took to No. 1 in the pop charts.

Decidedly less upbeat, "Frisco Line," by Shaffer and Bob (W.C.) Davis, follows a lonesome drifter who boards a Greyhound bus in Dallas, Texas, headed for San Francisco, California. The drifter sips from a bottle of wine, anticipating his arrival to a kind of paradise, compared with previous travels. But when the clouds of his mind dissipate, he realizes he left the big dog too early in Albuquerque, New Mexico. With a hint of drunken resolve, Mitchell's vocal fades to a whisper as he expresses dim hopes of starting a new life in an unexpected situation. "Frisco Line" marked the end of Mitchell's run on the *Billboard* charts. It was also Shaffer's most profound parable on life's twists and turns.

Yodeling Kenny Roberts' 1949 Coral Records hit, "I Never See Maggie Alone," boosted his career in radio and TV, earning jobs from Fort Wayne, Indiana, to burgs across the Midwest, including Saginaw, Michigan, where he hosted a kid's show on WNEM-TV during the mid-1960s. He and his family still lived in Saginaw when, in December of 1968, *Cash Box* reported on the novelty "Country Music Singing Sensation" with one word: "cute."[57] With robust enthusiasm, Roberts celebrates a poor boy's success from rags to rhinestone suits. The singer prevents an economic depression merely by paying his taxes. An album with the same title was Roberts' final long-player of three for Starday.

57. "Cash Box Country Roundup — Best Bets," *Cash Box* (New York City: December 14, 1968. Vol. 30, No. 20), 59.

Billy Golden. *Illustration by Craig Maki*

Billy Golden, a 30 year-old singer born in Alabama, started playing gigs on the west side of Detroit during the mid-1960s. He made a couple of singles issued on the local Walker, and Country Four labels, before cutting his second disc for Country Four, "Loser Making Good,"[58] in Nashville at Fred Foster Sound Studios, in late 1967. Featuring an earworm of a hook, the record's reception led to a contract with Starday, and Golden went from a regular guest at the "Big Country Jamboree" on WWVA radio Wheeling, West Virginia, to a full member — all while keeping a wife, and modest home in Taylor, Michigan.

58. "Loser Making Good" b/w "Life's Little Pleasures" by Billy Golden, Country Four CF 102, 1968, phonograph record. Also issued as "A Loser Makin' Good" on Starday 827 (single), 1968; and "Country Music's Golden Boy," Starday SLP 431 (album), 1968.

Golden's schedule included bookings at popular venues such as Club Canton, which was (still is)
Southeast Michigan's oldest honky tonk in continu-
ous operation. He appeared at local jamborees, and
toured taverns across Michigan, and bordering states.
His booking agent, Paul Wade, of Wayne, Michigan,
with the blessing of Nashville's original *Music City
News*, published a free regional circular titled *Music
City News – Michigan Supplement*, from 1966 through
1969. Early on, Golden wrote a "News and Notes"
fluff column for the magazine, until he hitched his
wagon to Starday, and his calendar filled up with gigs.

Wade wrote columns, too. In his "Round and
Bout'," of February 1968, he shared this tidbit:

> ... *Billy Golden, new Starday artist who hails from
> Taylor, Michigan, enjoying his biggest record, "I'm A
> Loser Making Good" [sp.]. Bill has chart action going
> for him in several markets and his bookings are coming
> in good. Recently played shows across Ohio, as well as
> Wisconsin and upper Michigan. When in town, he can
> be seen at Stanley's on VanBorn Road along with Red
> Ingle and Band.*[59]

Golden's first session at Starday Studios received
notice in Wade's column three months later:

> ... *Billy Golden cut four new sides at Starday a few
> weeks back and we've heard the tapes. Two of them are*

59. Paul Wade, "Round And Bout'," *Music City News – Michigan
Supplement* (Wayne, Michigan: February 1968, Vol. 3, No. 2), 10.
Lee "Red" Ingle helped produce Golden's Country Four records.

absolutely great, following "Loser Making Good" they have to be but I predict that the new one called "Wild Thing" [sp.] will hit big for Bill.[60]

Cash Box liked it, calling "Wild Wild Thing" "a fine, funky sound" and "a smooth, effective vocal effort."[61] The studio band builds drama by introducing new licks with different instruments at the clever turns of each verse, the words of which, combined with Golden's tough-as-nails delivery, drill into the listener's mind an unapologetic warning.

---

60. Paul Wade, "Round And Bout'," *Music City News – Michigan Supplement* (Wayne, Michigan: May 1968, Vol. 3, No. 5), 8.

61. "Best Bets," *Cash Box* (New York City: May 11, 1968. Vol. 29, No. 41), 56.

I was born on the breeze, raised beneath the trees
And the night the courthouse burned, they lost my name
I've got hot blood inside of this mountain of pride
And you're foolin' with a wild, wild thing

Go tell your mama
That you're foolin' with a wild, wild thing

I've got memories so unkind, they left scars on my mind
Cheatin' women and good booze have lost their sting
I'll hurt you 'til you cry, and I'll ramble 'til I die
And you're foolin' with a wild, wild thing [62]

The only hit was to Wade's expectations, as the song didn't chart. Starday released a couple more singles, but Golden could not hold the reins of his career, after the initial success. In the 1970s, he left Detroit for Tampa, Florida. By the early 1990s, Golden was living near San Bernardino, California. It seems he did, in fact, ramble 'til he died, at age 65 in Bullhead City, Arizona, in 2003. A dozen years later, while on a tour through Canada, Los Angeles musician and author Deke Dickerson discovered a copy of Golden's 1968 Starday album, "Country Music's Golden Boy," in a thrift shop. Immediately taken with "Wild Wild Thing," Dickerson revived the song as stripped-down rockabilly, pressed on a limited edition vinyl record. [63]

---

62. Dexter Shaffer - William Ellis, "Wild Wild Thing," Tarheel Music, BMI. 1968.

63. "Deke And The Whippersnappers" by Deke and the Whippersnappers, Pig Baby Records, PBR-018, 2017, extended play phonograph record.

In 1969, an album by Bobby Harden featuring "Except For One" (also issued as a single[64]), a Shaffer-Ellis country shuffle perfect for dancers on wooden sawdust-covered floors, included another notable Detroit connection. Producer Ralph Davis, originally from rural Wayne County, Tennessee, lived in Detroit during the 1950s, playing music with his two brothers as the Western Rhythm Boys. In 1957 the band cut Davis' self-penned "Undecided Heart," issued on Fortune Records subsidiary Hi-Q.[65] It didn't sell much,

64. "Except For One" b/w "The Wild Ones" by Bobby Harden, Starday 840, 1969, phonograph record.

65. "Undecided Heart" b/w "Searching For You" by Ralph Davis and Western Rhythm Boys, Hi-Q 15, 1957, phonograph record.

but raised his confidence. During the winter of 1959, Davis had had enough of Michigan's cold weather and moved to Nashville, where he worked in a print shop, and wrote and pitched songs in his spare time.

In 1960, Davis hired into the staff band at the "Grand Ole Opry" show as rhythm guitarist. In 1962, he joined Starday producers Pete Drake, and Tommy Hill at Window Music, through which Ernest Tubb, and Archie Campbell recorded his songs. Davis then met Bobby Harden, who performed with two sisters, Arlene and Robbie, as the Harden Trio. Originally from England, Arkansas, the act recorded in 1964-68 for Columbia Records. After the Harden Trio broke up, Davis worked with Bobby Harden on his Starday-King singles, and the album "Nashville Sensation."[66]

Also in 1969, Grady Leonard "Tiny" Harris recorded my favorite Shaffer-Ellis song, "Georgia Manhunt," which appeared as the B-side to a remake of Frankie Miller's 1959 hit "Black Land Farmer."[67] A race car driver, circus clown, disc jockey, and bandleader who spent his early life north of San Francisco in Ukiah, California, towering Tiny Harris also guest-starred on the stage of the "Grand Ole Opry," headlined at Las Vegas casinos, spent six months in Vietnam entertaining U.S. troops, and made records with the renowned Rose Maddox. Harris' endearing personality, broadened

---

66. "Nashville Sensation" by Bobby Harden, Starday SLPS-443, 1969, phonograph record. For more about Ralph Davis, see: Craig Maki. "Undecided Heart: Ralph Davis" (2017) https://www.carcitycountry.com/2017/undecided-heart-ralph-davis

67. "Georgia Manhunt" b/w "Black Land Farmer" by Tiny Harris, Starday 45-887, 1969, phonograph record.

through several episodes in entertainment, comes across in a way only a big man nicknamed "Tiny" can deliver: confident, without taking himself too seriously, selling every line with a wink. Most remarkably: "Georgia Manhunt" is a re-write of Vic Gallon's "I'm Gone" shellacked with a hard country veneer.

Loosely following the old song's melody, its lyrics tell about another man ready to travel across the country, only this time to escape a "sheriff and his posse, and them hound dogs" on his trail, all the while making plans to enjoy some sunshine, country ham, watermelon, and the company of women. Picture Vic Gallon burning rubber in 1957, and landing in a Georgia hoosegow. Then, after a dozen years behind bars, ducking out on a road trip of a different kind.

Harris' lowdown vocal pushes the groove at the
same tempo as Gallon's record, while a ferocious
guitar picker (a musical nod to Georgia native Jerry
Reed, perhaps) wails away, snapping the strings of an
acoustic flattop to their limits. Not a bad second life
for an obscure rockabilly record.

Other well-known artists who recorded Shaffer's
songs for Starday-King included George Morgan
("Country's Gone" — a rather poetic commentary
on suburban development, and its resulting loss of
farmland, and rural ways of life), Red Sovine (the
sing-songy "Live And Let Live And Be Happy"),
Charlie Walker ("Don't Put Down The Honky Tonks"
— a resurgent, hard-core country shuffle recorded
in 1971), Carl Tipton ("High Heels With No Soul"
— a bluegrass waltz not to be confused with songs
with similar titles cut by Johnny Paycheck, and Billy
Brown), and pop entertainers Arthur Prysock ("Frisco
Line"), and Roberta Sherwood ("To Wichita Falls
From L.A.," and "The Best Part Of My Years"), who
Shaffer personally enticed to sign with Starday in
1970.[68] (*For a list of Shaffer's works, see the Appendix.*)

"One time he came to [visit]," Kevin Legg said
about his uncle, "and we went to dinner. As he told
his stories, the entire restaurant was listening and
laughing. Tables stopped turning over, but nobody
seemed to mind. [He had a] simple Southern charm
with a wit for hypnotizing his audience … I suppose
that would be ingredients for writing a good song."

---

68. "Starday/King Signs 4 Names for Emerging Adult Market," *Cash Box* (New York City: January 24, 1970. Vol. 31, No. 26), 46.

Dexter Shaffer, Part IV

By 1970, Don Pierce, who'd spent the previous couple of years piecing together a deal to sell his business to the Lin Broadcasting Company, retired from Starday-King, leaving longtime manager Hal Neely an opening to step into the presidency. Neely named Shaffer "Western Regional Manager," and Shaffer and his wife moved to Southern California.

According to "Colonel" Jim Wilson, a vice president of Starday-King who, before joining the company in 1965, managed the King Records distribution office in Detroit starting in 1949, Shaffer "acted as an in-person liaison with our distributor there, and with the artists that we had."[69]

Born in Marion, Kentucky, and raised in Detroit, Wilson received a Kentucky Colonel title thanks to the political connections of his friend Bob Maxwell, a fellow Kentuckian, and radio broadcaster who worked at Detroit stations WJLB, WWJ, and WBRB (Mount Clemens) during the 1950s.[70] Wilson accepted a marketing job with Starday just a couple of years before it purchased King Records. Of Starday's man in California, Wilson said Shaffer helped coordinate productions, and facilitated contracts with talent based

---

69. "Colonel" Jim Wilson, interviewed by John Rumble, May 16, 1983, interview 19830516 OHC335, Country Music Foundation Oral History Project, Frist Library and Archive of the Country Music Hall of Fame and Museum, Nashville, TN.

70. "Bob Maxwell, 78; Radio Personality Also Worked in Film" *Los Angeles Times* (Los Angeles: January 4-5, 2003.), 163.

in the Southwest. Besides California, "any of our artists that were into the Vegas area, why Dexter would act as our representative there," explained Wilson.

In Las Vegas, Shaffer bargained with blue-eyed soul singer Wayne Cochran, a popular showman. In 1970, Cochran and his band the C.C. Riders cut two albums for Starday-King, one issued on King,[71] and the other on Starday's Bethlehem subsidiary,[72] with production assistance from musician John Wagner, who had built a recording studio during the previous decade in Albuquerque, New Mexico. Like Shaffer, Wagner began working with Starday-King in 1968. His group the John Wagner Foundation cut instrumentals "Blue In The Face" backed with "A Time For Love" for the Look label, a Starday-King subsidiary.[73]

In October 1970, Neely shared his views on the state of country music in *Record World* magazine. His forecast for Starday-King Records, and its publishing interests, would shift more attention to the Southwest:

… The most significant change in the entire country music scene is the emergence of a new country music style called "California Country." Starday has been quick to become a leader in signing and releasing these young

---

71. "Alive And Well And Living In A Bitch Of A World" by Wayne Cochran and The C.C. Riders, King KS-1116, 1970, phonograph record.

72. "High And Ridin'" by Wayne Cochran and The C.C. Riders, Bethlehem BS-10002, 1970, phonograph record.

73. "Blue In The Face" b/w "A Time For Love" by John Wagner Foundation, Look L-5031, 1968, phonograph record.

groups and now has in production and release singles and albums by Mayf Nutter, Hank and Lewie Wickam [sp.] and Gib Guilbeau and Swampwater. Getting its foothold in such showcases as the Troubadour Club in Los Angeles, this new music form will ... be the catalyst to truly make country music popular with the young people. Rock groups are tuning in as are the English groups to the "country sound and song." [74]

The style Neely tried to drive into the Starday-King stockade is known today as "country rock." By the mid-1960s, a trend of rock'n'roll musicians moving into the country music field (for example, Conway Twitty, Jerry Lee Lewis, Jack Scott, and Rick Nelson) influenced a younger generation to experiment with writing rock songs and arrangements that included instruments such as fiddles, and pedal steel guitar. Popular breakthroughs of the style included The Byrds' 1968 album "Sweetheart Of The Rodeo," and Rick Nelson and the Stone Canyon Band's 1969 "In Concert at the Troubadour" (the same club Neely called out in his piece). In the several years prior to Neely's op-ed, Starday-King's offerings of honky tonk and bluegrass music failed to score significant hits. Once Shaffer landed on the West Coast, it seems he began exploring the California country scene. Having written rockabilly songs a dozen years before, Shaffer may have sold the boss on pursuing country music combined with rock.

---

74. Hal Neely, "1970: A Key Year Of Growth," *Record World* (New York,: October 17, 1970. Vol. 25, No. 1218), 106.

Shaffer promoted the artists mentioned by Neely, many of whom played influential roles in Los Angeles at the time: Mayf Nutter, born in West Virginia, played guitar for rocker Del Shannon, and the New Christy Minstrels, before adding TV actor to his resumé. Gib Guilbeau collaborated with Gene Parsons, Linda Ronstadt, and The Flying Burrito Brothers.

Shaffer also served lesser-known talents such as Jack Kane, from Midland, Texas. Kane, a.k.a Jackson Kennelly, the bassist with Roy Orbison's first band the Teen Kings, made records distinguished by his gritty, yet expressive, deep voice. While the Vietnam War, citizen protests against it, and demonstrations for civil rights made headlines every day, the words of Kane's 1970 single for Look, "A Victim Of The Troubles On My Mind,"[75] written by Shaffer-Ellis, and produced by John Wagner, set in song the confusion many young people felt while pursuing meaning in American life:

I'm a child of the lost generation
And I'm searching for the things I can't find
I've got questions nobody wants to answer
I'm a victim of the troubles on my mind
...
Until freedom is an answer, not a question
I'll be a victim of the troubles on my mind [76]

---

75. "A Victim Of The Troubles On My Mind" b/w "Saginaw" by Jack Kane, Look 45-5030, 1970, phonograph record.
76. Dexter Shaffer - William Ellis, "A Victim Of The Troubles On My Mind," Tarheel Music, BMI. 1970.

Record label:

Playable On STEREO Or MONO

45-5030
Arranged By
Roger Jannotta
**Disc Jockey
Not for Sale**

634-L-5075
Tarheel (BMI)
Time: 2:17
Vocal
Produced By
John Wagner

LOOK RECORDS · DISTRIBUTED BY STARDAY · KING RECORDS, NASHVILLE, TENN.

A VICTIM OF THE TROUBLES ON MY MIND
(D. Shaffer–W. Ellis)
JACK KANE

Cash Box magazine suggested "Kane could get some play with this woeser."[77] Despite a modern, pop arrangement with electric guitar, soaring violins (not fiddles) and a horn section, the record failed to chart. With his unique voice, Kane went on to a successful career in advertising, with more singing, and film voiceovers. Wagner said he helped Kane sign with Look, and they undertook many musical adventures together, but Kane "never got hold of the brass ring."[78]

---

77. "Cash Box Country Singles — Best Bets," *Cash Box* (New York City: May 23, 1970. Vol. 31, No. 42), 54. We need to bring back the term "woeser."

78. Dick Stewart, *Fourteen Unsung Pioneers of Early Rock and Roll Who Didn't Get Their Due* (Xlibris: www.xlibris.com, 2020), 211.

Wagner also championed the country sound of brothers Hank and Lewie Wickham, investing his personal time, and resources in the act. "We started out with a small hit on 'Little Bit Late," he said.[79] After the brothers agreed to Wagner acting as their manager, and overseeing their recordings, "Dexter Shaffer of Starday and I worked very hard to get them to the right places," said Wagner.[80] He admitted, however, their product sold best in their home state of New Mexico. After a couple of years clamoring for a breakthrough, the act fell apart. By then, an unravelling at the top of Starday-King operations in Nashville made Shaffer a free agent.[81]

In October 1973, the Starday-King Records board announced a change of leadership, forcing out Neely, and his team.[82] After a dearth of hits during Neely's reign, Starday's next, and final success arrived in 1976, with Red Sovine's No. 1 hit "Teddy Bear."

Shaffer appeared to have not published another lyric, after the loss of his role for Starday-King. He stayed in California, and took on sales for Wagner's production company, which had completed a few

---

79. "Little Bit Late" b/w "Endless Love Affair" by Lewie Wickham, Starday 45-888, 1970, phonograph record. Entertainer Jim Stafford performed the song on the Smothers Brothers television show, providing a brief boost to the Wickhams' and Wagner's careers.

80. Stewart, op. cit., 202.

81. To read more about Starday records, see: Nathan D. Gibson, *The Starday Story – The House that Country Music Built* (Oxford, Mississippi: University Press of Mississippi, 2011).

82. "Shepherd Named Starday-King G.M." *Cash Box* (New York City: October 20, 1973. Vol. 35, No. 18), 8.

projects for Frank Zappa's management firm Third
Story Music when Motown Records (recently moved
to Los Angeles from Detroit, calling its new offices
Motown West) invited Wagner to produce artists
for its Natural Resources label. Wagner worked on
albums by a blues rock band called Heart (not the
1980s rock stars), and a fiddler named Corliss Nelson.[83] In 1973, Motown released a single by the John
Wagner Coalition on its Rare Earth label, "The Battle
Is Over," an anti-war ballad with wispy vocals and
softly played acoustic guitar in a combination that
reminds one of ancient English folk music.[84]

Also in 1973, after a lifetime of playing guitar,
including with the main studio lineup at Motown
Records during part of its golden era, and scoring a
top ten hit in 1971 with his instrumental "Scorpio"
on Sussex Records, Dennis Coffey moved his family
from Detroit to the Los Angeles suburb of Canoga
Park, in the San Fernando Valley. According to Coffey, L.A. was filled with more opportunities to earn
a living in the music business than anywhere he'd
traveled. Besides performing on countless stages, and
recording sessions, Coffey wrote, produced, and arranged music. While co-managing a production company, he contracted work at Motown West, played on
film, and television soundtracks, and performed with
stars, and up-and-comers alike.

---

83. Stewart, op. cit., 206.
84. "The Battle Is Over" b/w "Take Time To Love Me" by The John
    Wagner Coalition, Rare Earth R 5051F, 1973, phonograph record.

Coffey spent three years living in L.A., before returning to Michigan. Then he tried New York City, but after a couple of years, he settled for good in the Detroit area. He didn't mention whether he'd crossed paths with Shaffer — or Wagner, for that matter — while in California. If he had, maybe the circumstances did not make an impression worth noting.

In the weeks after the end of Hal Neely's Starday-King presidency, Shaffer's former co-writer William Ellis made connections with song publishers Hill and Range, and Shotgun Music.[85] His path in the song business trailed off from there. Ellis died north of Nashville in Ashland City, Tennessee, in 2004, at age 64.

D.V. Shaffer passed away in Santa Barbara, California, in 1991, at the age of 59. "Mom always said the drinking was what led to an early death," said nephew Kevin Legg. An obituary stated Shaffer had been vice president of sales and marketing for John Wagner Productions.[86] He was laid to rest in a family cemetery plot in South Charleston, West Virginia. Seven years later, at 80 years old, Lillian Delita Myers joined Shaffer at his heavenly party.

---

85. "Miss Bledsoe Becomes Bride," *The Commercial Appeal* (Memphis, Tennessee: August 7, 1974. Vol. 135, No. 219), 11.

86. Obituary notice for Dexter V. Shaffer, *Charleston Gazette* (Charleston, West Virginia: December 8, 1991).

COMPLIMENTARY
GONDOLA

DEE JAY   SPECIAL

PROMOTION   NOT
COPY   FOR SALE
Vocal By   Vic Gallon

HIGH FIDELITY   De-Shaf: BMI
                                Time: 2:31
                                45-G1414-2

I'M GONE(ALT)
(Shaffer-Myers)
Vic Gallon

The recently pressed facsimile Gondola 45 rpm record features
two recordings of "I'm Gone"— the original made at Northwest
Sound, and the alternate version (pictured) for Mercury Records.
Label scheme: white paper with black ink.

Vic Gallon, Part III

About a dozen years ago, lacquer-coated discs of Shaffer's Mercury recording session, traced back to Ernie Durham, turned up for sale. The discs had no paper labels; just song titles scrawled in grease pencil near the spindle holes, without noting the artist, or record company. A British collector who bought the discs recognized Vic Gallon's song, "I'm Gone." Wishing to share this exciting discovery, the buyer made public this "alternate" version on a couple of compilations of 1950s rock'n'roll made in Europe.[87] The popularity of this mystery music also inspired the manufacture of a new 45 rpm single with facsimile Gondola labels that paired the original Northwest Sound recording of "I'm Gone" on one side, with the newly discovered version on its flip.[88] Because the demo disc didn't indicate a source, every new publication of it was credited to Vic Gallon.

The performance sounded like dynamite, despite its poor audio quality. No one seemed to know its true origins (record company, musicians, and circumstances), so I began a hunt to discover the details.

Having found no trace of Vic Gallon in old address books, census records, music journals, or

87. "Desperate Rock And Roll, Vol. 21" by Various Artists, Flame 021, 2009, phonograph album.
   "Rock'N'Roll Orgy, Vol. 9" by Various Artists, Flesh Den 6909, 2009, compact disc.
88. "I'm Gone" b/w "I'm Gone (ALT)" by Vic Gallon, Gondola G1414 (reproduction), ca. 2010, phonograph record.

interviews with contemporaries, I turned my attention to Shaffer the songwriter. A 1968 report in a music industry magazine noted Shaffer was a "former artist for Mercury."[89] This clue led me to find the particulars of Shaffer's 1957 Mercury session in Chicago. Listed just below an entry for pop singer Nick Noble, Shaffer's session included "unissued" recordings of "I'm Gone," and "I'll Keep Loving You" [sp.] (*as described in "Dexter Shaffer Part II"*).

After picking my jaw off the floor, and setting it back to its natural grin, I listened again to the two versions of "I'm Gone" pressed on the new 45, and then compared the alternate take of "I'm Gone" with Nick Noble's "Sweet Treat" — and a burst from above sent spears of lightning crackling into the depths of my ocean of notions. The truth had been there, all along: Vic Gallon and Dexter Shaffer were the same man — making "I'm Gone" the most aptly titled tune, ever.

Although Shaffer's session is listed after Noble's, the numerical order of the Mercury matrices of completed takes suggests Shaffer's recordings were done *in the middle of* Noble's session.[90] Close listening affirms the alternate take of "I'm Gone" features instrumentation identical to that heard on Noble's "Sweet Treat" — piano, two electric guitars, bass, and drums. Furthermore, the music of both songs sounds

---

89. See note 53.

90. Ruppli and Novitsky, op. cit. , 115. Consider the order of these matrices: Nick Noble = 16046 ("Sweet treat"), 16047 ("Halo of love"), 16048 ("Baby, I don't like it"), 16051 ("You are the gold of my heart"); Dexter Shaffer = 16049 ("I'm gone"), 16050 ("I'll keep loving you"). Both session entries include "Orchestra & Chorus cond. by Carl Stevens. Universal Recording Studios, Chicago, 1957."

so similar, the prod of obsession forced me to run out my door to locate an original copy of Noble's 45 … Aaaannd I'm back … Another spin of the records reveals the drummer on both "Sweet Treat" and "I'm Gone," pops the same tempo, the guitarists pick variations of the same licks, and the pianist pounds the same ground. The vocal chorus on Noble's recording does not appear on "I'm Gone," but may have harmonized through Shaffer's take of "I'll Keep Loving You" — I don't know, as it's not been made public.[91]

Furthermore, here's where we witness how real rock'n'roll laughs last: Noble's vocal for "Sweet Treat" bops along with the band swinging lightly and pleasantly; whereas when he opens his big mouth, Shaffer sings like his survival depends on it, and the band responds.

He belts, shouts, gasps, sneers — slurring his words, allowing some notes to slide into guttural sobs — there's no way he's standing still while expending this kind of mania. The band goes from sunny and mild when backing Noble, to wild and dangerous, dragging us along for a delirious ride with Shaffer at the wheel. And before the recording volume begins its slow fade toward the end, a frenzied Shaffer — aware of just seconds left in the performance of his lifetime — takes a final shot at making his rock'n'roll reputation. — He doesn't let up, but *lengthens the take* by chanting over the music, "Well, REEALLL GONE! Uh huh, GONE! Well, MAma, GONE! YEEeaaaAAH, GONE!"

---

91. Perhaps the chorus, which sounds like the Anita Kerr Singers on Noble's record, performs hand claps during "I'm Gone."

Mercury chose Noble's recordings for release, but thanks to a cryptic disc without labels, saved for decades by the celebrated Ernie Durham in his kitty of ditties, twenty-first century music lovers prefer digging Shaffer's gem of a performance — A final gift from the Frantic One, to rock'n'rollers everywhere.

Judging by Noble's record, the original source of Shaffer's Mercury tracks must sound stellar. The current state of the audio is so poor, likely due to disc wear, and aging of its lacquer surface, that hearing it is like looking at an ancient snapshot obscured by fading, fingerprints, and corner creases. Because of this, some fans speculated it was a demo older than the Gondola session. I'm shocked the track hasn't been released before, considering how, over the last five decades, American and European researchers have combed through old tape libraries to harvest unissued rock'n'roll music. Could Shaffer's master recordings still await rediscovery on the reel of Noble's session for "Sweet Treat?" It may sound far-fetched that a company such as Mercury would allow it, but D.V. Shaffer, who could quiet a busy restaurant filled with strangers by telling amusing tales about his life, might have talked Carl Stevens into letting him leave Universal Recording Studios with the tape of his session in hand.

Before he arrived in Detroit, Shaffer probably followed his own path, re-inventing himself as needed. No doubt, it helped him survive the constant dog-eat-dog conditions of music, and sales professions. The recent "return" of Vic Gallon, when the 1957 Mercury session first appeared on this side of the millenium, and its acceptance by devotees as simply another early rock'n'roll enigma, extended Shaffer's saga of creative renewal. It also cooked up new food for thought.

Clearly, the Gondola record was meant to launch the Shaffer-Myers song writing team, and De-Shaf song publishing company. Considering the eight-month economic recession that began in August 1957, was the move to Chicago, and the Mercury session an attempt for a clean break? Did he consider the Vic Gallon episode a mistake? Seventy years later, listening to his marvelous rock'n'roll, this admirer would beg to differ.

Did Shaffer mean to evade scrutiny by making and promoting his record with the name Vic Gallon? Considering the population density of Detroit during the 1950s, and the closeness and size of its music community, it would have been difficult to get away with the ruse for long. Yet "Vic Gallon" had the nerve to appear on one of the most listened-to country music radio shows in town.

I found no evidence of public performances by Gallon (or Shaffer) in Detroit. If he did take a stage, it was probably as a guest with another band, rather than leading one of his own.

Finally, whence did the name Vic Gallon originate? Most singers kept their first names when they adopted stage monikers (e.g., Johnny Powers, and Jack Scott). Having been married to Mexican Lewis Martinez, Delita Myers probably knew some Spanish. Vic Gallon might have been an affectionate translation of "victorio galán," or the "handsome victory" of her man. It's a stretch — but entertaining, no?

Epilogue - I'm Gone

In 2014, a *collectionneur de disques* from France visiting a retired record dealer in Florida landed a seven-inch lacquer coated disc sporting Northwest Recording Laboratories labels (yes, *our* Northwest). Details of the record, outtakes of "I'm Gone" (including a false start), and "I Keep Lovin' You," from the Gondola session, had been typed on its paper labels. The name "Dexter Schaefer" appears, with no mention of Vic Gallon. (Note the spelling of Shaffer's name reads the same as the busy Detroit highway.) Does "Sept. 1, 1957," also typed on the labels, indicate the day of the Gondola recording session (a Sunday), or simply the day Skinner happened to make the disc? As of this writing, these takes remain unpublished. Something to look forward to.

I wouldn't be surprised to hear someone attempted to link Shaffer the songwriter to Vic Gallon's identity, after this find. However, the Frenchman announced the seller said he got the record from Shaffer himself, who, the man claimed, worked for Northwest Sound. This tidbit may have thrown people off Vic Gallon's trail. However, in 1953, Northwest Sound retained a salesman, so it's plausible Shaffer held the same position.[92] No one else has hinted at Shaffer's employment while he lived in Detroit. In fact, it would have been an easy car ride to the house on Ardmore from Shaffer's apartment — especially with the back-seat speaker "settin' on a rock billy song."

---

92. See note 8. The salesman's name was Jay McFadden.

RECORDING NORTHWEST LABORATORIES

"I'LL BE GONE"
Dexter Scheafer
Sept 1, 1957
J. Skinner Eng.

14958 ARDMORE DETROIT 27, MICH. BRoadway 3-7804

RECORDING NORTHWEST LABORATORIES

"I"LL KEEP ON LOVEN YOU"
Dexter Scheafer
Sept 1, 1957
J. Shinner Eng.

14958 ARDMORE DETROIT 27, MICH. BRoadway 3-7804

Appendix

WORKS BY DEXTER SHAFFER
(PUBLISHING AND RECORDINGS NOTED)

Unpublished, 1956
"Fairy Land Of Love"
Dexter Shaffer - Delita Myers

Vic Gallon
"I'm Gone"
"I Keep Lovin' You"
Dexter Shaffer - Delita Myers, De-Shaf Music - BMI
Gondola G-14141, 1957 (single)

Dexter Shaffer
"I'm Gone"
"I'll Keep Loving You" [sp.]
Dexter Shaffer - Delita Myers, De-Shaf Music - BMI
Unissued Mercury session with Carl Stevens Orchestra, 1957
"I'm Gone" manufactured 2009 on rock'n'roll compilations pro-duced overseas (see note 85), and one side of a facsimile Gondola seven-inch record (see page 56). In all instances, the track is credited to Vic Gallon, and labeled an alternate take.

Shaffer Productions
Narrated by Art Mercier, with Russ Gaede, and
Tom McNally
"Game Calling In Hi-Fi, Vol. 1"
Mercury GC-100, 1960 (album)
Copyright Dexter V. Shaffer

COMPLIMENTARY
GONDOLA

DEE JAY   SPECIAL

PROMOTION   NOT
COPY   FOR SALE
Vocal By   Vic Gallon

Orchestration: HIGH FIDELITY
D. Coffey   De-Shaf: BMI
L. Blockno   Time 2:34
L. Stage   45-G1414-2

I KEEP LOVIN' YOU
(Shaffer-Myers)
Vic Gallon

Billy Golden
"Wild Wild Thing"
Dexter Shaffer - William Ellis, Tarheel - BMI
Produced by Al Gore
Starday 840, 1968 (single)
Starday SLP-431, "Country Music's Golden Boy," 1968
(album)

Guy Mitchell
"Frisco Line"
Bob Davis - Dexter Shaffer, Starday - BMI
Produced by Thomas Wayne and Hal Neely
Starday 846, 1968 (single)
Starday LP-432, "Singin' Up A Storm," 1968 (album)
Starday NLP 2074, "Heartaches By The Number," 1970
(album)

Kenny Roberts
"Country Music Singing Sensation"
Dexter Shaffer - William Ellis, Tarheel - BMI
Produced by Jack Linneman and Al Gore
Starday 851, 1968 (single)
Starday SLP-434, "Country Music Singing Sensation,"
1968 (album)

Red Sovine
"Live And Let Live And Be Happy"
Dexter Shaffer - William Ellis, Tarheel - BMI
Produced by Tommy Hill
Starday 852, 1968 (single)
Starday SLP 441, "Closing Time 'Til Dawn," 1969 (album)

George Morgan
"Live And Let Live And Be Happy"
Dexter Shaffer - William Ellis, Tarheel - BMI
Produced by Tommy Hill
Starday 860, 1969 (single)
"Frisco Line"
Bob Davis - Dexter Shaffer, Starday - BMI
"Country's Gone"
Dexter Shaffer - William Ellis, Tarheel - BMI
Starday SLP 435, "Sounds Of Goodbye," 1969 (album)
[*SLP 435 produced by Don Pierce. Dexter Shaffer is credited author of liner notes.*]

Lois Williams
"Castle Of Shame" (with Red Sovine)
Dexter Shaffer - William Ellis, Tarheel-BMI
Produced by Louie Innis
Starday SLP 448, "A Girl Named Sam," 1969 (album)
"He's The Man" (also Starday 873, 1969 (single))
John Mohr - Dexter Shaffer, Tarheel-BMI

Roy Drusky
"Country's Gone"
Dexter Shaffer - William Ellis, Tarheel-BMI
Produced by Jerry Kennedy
Mercury SR-61206, "A Portrait Of Roy Drusky," 1969
(album)

Gene Dunlap
"One Brick At A Time"
Dexter Shaffer - William Ellis, Tarheel-BMI
Produced by [Jack] Hoss Linneman and Al Gore
Starday 870, 1969 (single)

Bobby Harden
"Except For One"
Dexter Shaffer - William Ellis, Tarheel-BMI
Produced by Ralph Davis
Starday 875, 1969 (single)
Starday SLPS-443, "Nashville Sensation," 1969 (album)

Tiny Harris
"Georgia Manhunt"
Dexter Shaffer - William Ellis, Tarheel-BMI
Produced by William Ellis
Starday 887, 1969 (single)

Arthur Prysock
"Frisco Line"
W.C. Davis - Dexter Shaffer, Starday-BMI
Produced by Hal Neely and William Ellis
Starday 954, 1972 (single)
King KSD-1064, "The Country Side of Arthur Prysock,"
1969 (album)

Carl Tipton
"High Heels With No Soul"
Dexter Shaffer - William Ellis, Tarheel-BMI
Produced by William Ellis
Starday 894, 1970 (single)

Jack Kane
"A Victim Of The Troubles On My Mind"
Dexter Shaffer - William Ellis, Tarheel-BMI
Produced by John Wagner
Look 45-5030, 1970 (single)

Roberta Sherwood
"To Wichita Falls From L.A."
Dexter Shaffer, Tarheel-BMI
Produced by Dexter Shaffer and Hal Neely
King 45-6387, 1970 (single)
"The Best Part Of My Years"
Dexter Shaffer - William Ellis, Tarheel-BMI
King 45-6343, 1972 (single)
King KLP-1112 "This Good Life," 1971 (album)

Howard Stansell
"Country's Gone"
Dexter Shaffer - William Ellis, Tarheel-BMI
Produced by John Wagner
Look 45-5028, 1970 (single)

Judy West
"Nashville Wives"
Dexter Shaffer - William Ellis, Tarheel-BMI
Produced by Darrell Glenn
Starday 906, 1970 (single)

Charlie Walker
"Don't Put Down The Honky Tonks"
Dexter Shaffer - William Ellis, Tarheel-BMI
Produced by Billy Sherrill
Epic 30660, "Honky Tonkin' With Charlie Walker" 1971
(album)

Mayf Nutter
"Nashville Wives" / "Country's Gone"
Dexter Shaffer - William Ellis, Tarheel-BMI (*both titles*)
Produced by John Wagner
Starday 922, 1971 (single)

Discography

NORTHWEST SOUND COMPANY
14958 Ardmore, Detroit, Michigan 48227

Jimmy Mack "D"
1960. Phonograph record, 45 rpm. Backed by Nick Harris
and the Soundbarriers. Rock'n'roll.
NSC-1001...She's Got It! [R. Dunkley - J. Dunkley]
 Dunkley Music Pub. (BMI)
NSC-1002...Yes, It's True [R. Dunkley - J. Dunkley]
 Dunkley Music Pub. (BMI)

Nick Harris and the Soundbarriers
1960. Phonograph record, 45 rpm. Instrumental rock'n'roll.
NSC-1003...Big Nick [N. Harris - A. Punturi]
 True Tone Pub. Co. (BMI)
NSC-1004...Music, Music, Music [Weiss - Baum]
 Cromwell Music Corp. (ASCAP)

Leroy Ali
1961. Phonograph record, 45 rpm. Pop.
NSC-1005...Dreamer [L. Ali] Dunkley Music Pub. (BMI)
NSC-1005...Late Show Can Cha [L. Ali] Dunkley Music
 Pub. (BMI)

Dean-O-DelRay and his DelRays
1963. Phonograph record, 45 rpm. Rock'n'roll.
NSC-1007...I Want To Be Your Lucky Star
 [Oscar Davidson]
 Roman Music Pub. Co. (BMI)
NSC-1007...The Ballad Of Billy The Kid
 [Oscar Davidson]
 Roman Music Pub. Co. (BMI)

Dennis Jorden
1964. Phonograph record, 45 rpm. Rock'n'roll.
NSC-1008...Since I Met You Baby [Ivory Joe Hunter]
         Progressive Music (BMI)
NSC-1008...Any Message [Dennis J. Bejester]
         Skintone Music Co. (BMI)

The Checkmates
1964. Phonograph record, 45 rpm. Rock'n'roll.
NSC-1009...West Side Whizz (Vocal) [Daniel A. Jakary]
         Skintone Music Co. (BMI)
NSC-1009...West Side Whizz (Instrumental)
         [Daniel A. Jakary] Skintone Music Co. (BMI)

Die Contetts
1968. Phonograph record, 45 rpm. German. Labels state
"Recorded in West Germany."
1001.............He-He-He De-Ef-Be [Peter Wobst]
             Skintone Music Co. (BMI)
1001.............Sonntags Geht's Sum Fussballplatz (Sundays
             We Go To The Soccer Field) [Peter Wobst]
             Skintone Music Co. (BMI)

Elder G.D. Moore "The Light Of The Glorious Gospel."
1968. Phonograph album, 33 1/3 rpm. Religious.
1011 LP.......Side 1: Scripture
1011 LP.......Side 2: Sermon

ROMAN
RECORDS

Lyndale Music
Co. - BMI
ZTSC-84263

Record #1010
Time; 2:15
45 rpm

PREACHIN' TALK
(R. Cohen - T. Moers)
ROY CORWIN

ROMAN RECORDS

Roy Corwin
1961. Phonograph record, 45 rpm. Pop.
1010.............Preachin' Talk [Roy Cohen - Tommy Moers]
                Lyndale Music Co. (BMI)
1010.............Look Out [Roy Cohen - Tommy Moers]
                Catalina Music (BMI); Lovelane Music

Vibrato's
1961. Phonograph record, 45 rpm. Instrumental rock'n'roll.
This group appears to include members of the Tremelos on
Raco Records 1120 (1962), and Thunderbolt Records 100
(1963).
2020.............Summer Love [I. Horvath - J. Horvath -
                R. Chabane] Dunkley Music (BMI)
2020.............Pancho [I. Horvath - J. Horvath - R. Cirrate]
                Dunkley Music (BMI)

Neil Morelli
1964. Phonograph record, 45 rpm. Doo wop.
3030.............She Broke My Heart [N. Morelli - Y. Cadoret]
                Skintone Music (BMI)
3030.............She Broke My Heart (Instrumental)
                [N. Morelli - Y. Cadoret]
                Skintone Music (BMI)

The Monarchs
1966. Phonograph record, 45 rpm. Garage rock.
4040.............Days Gone By [M. Russell]
                Skintone Music (BMI)
4040.............Needles And Pins [Bono - Nitzsche]
                Metric Music (BMI)

Bibliography

Coffey, Dennis. *Guitars, Bars, and Motown Superstars.* Ann Arbor: University of Michigan Press, 2004.

Gibson, Nathan D. *The Starday Story — The House that Country Music Built.* Oxford, Mississippi: University Press of Mississippi, 2011.

Maki, Craig. *Tomorrow Brings Memories: Detroit's First Underground Record Company.* Beverly Hills, Michigan: Wax Hound Press, 2022.

Maki, Craig, with Keith Cady. *Detroit Country Music: Mountaineers, Cowboys, and Rockabillies.* Ann Arbor: University of Michigan Press, 2013.

Miller, Billy, and Michael Hurtt. *Mind Over Matter: The Myths & Mysteries of Detroit's Fortune Records.* New York City: Kicks Books, 2020.

Ruppli, Michel, and Ed Novitsky. *The Mercury Labels: A Discography, Volume II, The 1956–1964 Era.* Germany: Greenwood Press, 1993.

Stewart, Dick. *Fourteen Unsung Pioneers of Early Rock and Roll Who Didn't Get Their Due.* Xlibris: www.xlibris.com, 2020.

"Colonel" Jim Wilson, interview by John Rumble. May 16, 1983. Interview 19830516 OHC335. Country Music Foundation Oral History Project. Frist Library and Archive of the Country Music Hall of Fame and Museum, Nashville, TN.

Listening suggestions

Jimmy Kirkland. *Cool Daddy*. Rollercoaster Records –
RCCD 3054 (England), 2007. Compact disc. [Tracks
from Northwest Sound sessions (incl. Johnny Powers)]

Johnny Powers. *Long Blond Hair*. Norton Records – ED-229
(USA), 1992. Phonograph record, 33⅓ rpm; and compact
disc. [Tracks recorded at Northwest Sound Company]

Various. *Desperate Rock And Roll, Vol. 21*. Flame – 021
(England), 2009. Phonograph record, 33⅓ rpm. [Dexter
Shaffer's Mercury session (credited to Vic Gallon)]

Various. *The Michigan Box*. Be! Sharp Records – 6068-77
(Germany), 2015. Compact disc (box of ten). [Vic Gal-
lon, Nick Harris, and Dean-O Delray tracks recorded at
Northwest Sound Company]

HANDSOME VICTORY PLAYLIST

Use the camera on your cell phone to scan the QR code
for the author's hand-picked "Handsome Victory Playlist"
hosted by Wax Hound Press on YouTube.

You may also access it with this Web address:
https://bit.ly/3KgSvEG

Index

Acknowledgments

My immense gratitude to the following people for their attention, and enthusiasm for this project: Mark Lee Allen, Sven Bergmann, Keith Cady, Loney Charles, Deke Dickerson, John Fabke, Chris Flanagan, Nathan D. Gibson, Michael Hurtt, Barney Koumis, Ray Moers, and Pascal Perrault. Special thanks to Kevin Legg. Cheers to the folks who unearthed these discs, believed in the music, and shared it with the world. My sincere respect to all.

Much appreciation for these taxpayer- and member-supported institutions: the Baldwin Public Library of Birmingham, Michigan; the University of Michigan Library of Ann Arbor, Michigan; and the Frist Library and Archive of the Country Music Hall of Fame and Museum of Nashville, Tennessee.

Many thanks to my family.

www.ingramcontent.com/pod-product-compliance
Lightning Source LLC
Chambersburg PA
CBHW072206090426
42740CB00012B/2414